LITTLE FOLK

LITTLE FOLK

STORIES FROM AROUND THE WORLD

Paul Robert Walker

ILLUSTRATED BY

James Bernardin

Harcourt Brace & Company

San Diego   New York   London

To Dariel Anne Walker,
my littlest little folk

—P. R. W.

To Christopher, Hannah, and Claire,
three little folks who have made
this world a more magical place

—J. B.

Text copyright © 1997 by Paul Robert Walker
Illustrations copyright © 1997 by James Bernardin

"People of the Rock" adapted from *Zulu Fireside Tales* by Phyllis Savory,
published by Howard Timmins, Cape Town, 1961.

Library of Congress Cataloging-in-Publication Data
Walker, Paul Robert.
Little folk: stories from around the world/by Paul Robert Walker;
illustrated by James Bernardin.—1st ed.   p.   cm.
Includes bibliographical references (p. 68).
Contents: Rumpelstiltskin (Germany)—One-inch boy (Japan)—My friend,
the nisse (Denmark)—The capture of summer (North America)—People of
the rock (South Africa)—The golden ball (Wales)—Laka and the Menehune
(Hawaiian Islands)—The red-ribbon leprechaun (Ireland)
ISBN 0-15-200327-4
1. Tales.   2. Fairies—Folklore.   3. Leprechauns—Folklore.   4. Dwarfs—
Folklore.   [1. Fairies—Folklore.   2. Leprechauns—Folklore.   3. Dwarfs—
Folklore.   4. Folklore.]   I. Bernardin, James, ill.   II. Title.
PZ8.1.W1287Li   1997
398.2—dc20   [E]   96-2456

First edition
A C E F D B

Printed in Mexico

The illustrations in this book were done in acrylic and colored pencil on paper.
The display type was set in Retablo Antiguo and Village.
The text type was set in Minion by Thompson Type, San Diego, California.
Color separations by Bright Arts, Ltd., Singapore
Printed and bound by RR Donnelley & Sons Company, Reynosa, Mexico
This book was printed on Patina Matte paper.
Production supervision by Stanley Redfern
Designed by Lydia D'moch

Contents

LITTLE FOLK

Author's Note

Not so long ago, they shared our world—dancing among the rocks and trees, tucked away in the hayloft, appearing and disappearing in the time it takes to turn around. Our great-great-great-grandparents knew them well, for there were more in their days than in ours. Or perhaps it only seems that way. Perhaps they are among us still, watching from the rafters or the corners of the room, peeping out from under the bushes, laughing at the strange, big ways of the human race.

They're known by countless names: fairy, dwarf, elf, and leprechaun; pixie, brownie, and hobgoblin; nisse, Menehune, and nunu. They are the little folk, and they've inspired delightful stories all over the world. In this book I retell eight of these stories, representing a wide variety of cultures, from Japan to Denmark, from the Zulu of South Africa to the Wabanaki of North America.

1

Although there is wonderful variety among the tales, there are also striking similarities. As with other folktales, the same basic story is often told by people who are widely separated by geography and language. For example, the Japanese folktale of Issun Boshi—which I have retold as "One-Inch Boy"—is remarkably similar to the English folktale of Tom Thumb. And both these tales echo stories told in many other lands.

There are equally intriguing connections among very different stories. The dwarfs of Europe, the Menehune of Hawaii, the nunus of the Zulu, and the little folk of many North American Indian tribes all live in rocks and caves. Before they lived in caves, the Menehune were protectors of the forest, while European fairies, Irish leprechauns, and Wabanaki dwarfs are all associated with trees and bushes.

Perhaps the most interesting connection, however, is that tales of little folk are told as if they *really happened.* In a similar book called *Giants!* I told tales from a distant past, a time before time, when great heroes battled the old race of giants. Tales of little folk are different. They come from a more recent "long ago," a time not so different from our own.

In the early nineteenth century, when T. Crofton Croker gathered folktales in southern Ireland, he met people who claimed to have seen a leprechaun with their own eyes. During the same period, Danish farmers told stories about the elflike nisse, who, they said, lived on specific, nearby farms. Less than a century ago, Hawaiians still pointed out structures built by the Menehune, while the Zulu could point to a rock where the nunus lived.

Why are tales of little folk more "real" than tales of giants? Is it possible that the little folk themselves are more real? Or that they *were* more real?

Of course, there have always been people who are smaller than others, just as there are people who are taller. And in earlier times, these different-sized people were often believed to have magical powers, a superstition that probably influenced the tales of little folk.

The great anthropologist W. Y. Evans-Wentz—who studied the "fairy faith" in Ireland, Scotland, and Wales—thought that, on the surface, some tales may reflect whole races of smaller people, past or present. In the British Isles, the early Picts were smaller than later Celtic people, while taller African tribes like the Zulu had contact with small-statured tribes like the Bushmen and Pygmies. But, as Evans-Wentz pointed out, stories of little folk are also told in places where there never was a "pygmy" race, and smaller races of today have their own tales of little folk, so the real roots must lie deeper.

He suggested that little folk may represent a primitive concept of the human soul, imagined as a tiny version of the body. Or perhaps they are spirits of the dead, which would explain their ghostlike quality of appearing and disappearing in the blink of an eye. Some Christian cultures see them as fallen angels, exiled from heaven. Yet others see them as pagan house gods or nature spirits, symbols of the earth itself, an idea that echoes their close connection with rocks and trees.

Whatever the origin of the little folk, storytellers have used a good dose of imagination to create a delightful body of tales about them. In researching these tales, I have tried to peel away the layers of time, going back to the earliest available written texts of each story. I've detailed these sources—along with my thanks to those who helped me find them—in the notes that follow each tale. But I would like to offer a special thanks here to Diane Zwemer, who helped me locate early texts of many different tales in the libraries of UCLA.

Even the earliest text, however, is only a snapshot in time, reflecting the way the story was told on a particular day by a particular person and, further, the way that story was written down, often in more polished form, by yet another person. So, while respecting my sources, I have also used my own imagination, combining elements from similar stories, creating dialogue, developing characters, and adding twists of plot. My goal has always been to give life to these stories today—for the little folk who read them, for the little folk laughing in the shadows, for the little folk inside us all.

—P. R. W.

Rumpelstiltskin

Germany

Once there was a man who owned a mill. All day he worked at the big stone wheel, grinding wheat and rye into flour for baking bread. It was a hard life, and as he worked at the wheel, the poor miller dreamed of being a great and wealthy man. But more than this, he dreamed of a brilliant future for his beautiful daughter.

Now it happened that one day the king of that country passed through the miller's town. As the royal carriage rolled by, the miller loudly boasted of his daughter's beauty and talents. "Why, she can even spin straw into gold!" he proclaimed.

When the king heard the miller's words, he ordered the carriage stopped—for he was very fond of gold. "If what you say is true," he said, "I will marry your daughter and make her my queen. Bring her to my castle tomorrow, and I'll put her to the test. But I warn you, old man, if she fails I'll chop off her head."

The miller's heart swelled with pride at the prospect of his daughter marrying the king. *As for spinning straw into gold,* he thought, *surely the king will forget all about it when he sees my daughter's beauty.*

The next day, the miller brought his daughter to the castle, but though the king was indeed impressed by her beauty, he was far more impressed by the promise of gold. So he sent the foolish miller home and led the miller's daughter into a room full of straw, with nothing else but a wooden chair and a spinning wheel.

"Now get to work," he ordered, "and spin all night. If the straw is not spun into gold by dawn, I'll chop off your head." With that, he closed the door behind him and left the miller's daughter all alone.

The poor girl sat on the hard wooden chair and gazed at the room full of straw. Of course, she didn't have the slightest idea how to spin straw into gold; in fact, she didn't know much about spinning at all. "What will I do?" she moaned. "He'll have my head for sure." And she began to sob until the straw grew damp with her tears.

Suddenly the door opened and a strange little man hopped into the room. "Why are you crying, Mistress Miller?" he asked.

"Oh!" she sighed, "I must spin this straw into gold or the king will chop off my head."

"What's so hard about that?" he asked.

"What's so hard?" she asked back. "What's so hard is that it's impossible!"

"Not impossible! Not impossible!" he chanted, dancing around the room. "Not impossible for me!"

The miller's daughter stared at the strange little man. He was ugly and weird, but there was something about him just the same—something magical. "Could you really do it?" she asked.

"For a price!" he sang. "A price! A price!"

The young woman undid the clasp of her necklace and offered it to the little man. "Will you do it for this?"

"Done!" he cried, snatching the necklace from her outstretched hand. Then he sat beside the spinning wheel and went to work. *Whirr! Whirr! Whizz!* In the blink of an eye, the spool was full of golden thread. He put on another spool and another and another, until all the straw in the room had been spun to gold.

The next morning, when the king opened the door, his eyes flashed with joy at the shimmering gold. But the joy quickly turned to greed, and that night he led the miller's daughter into a larger room full of straw. "If the straw is not spun to gold," he threatened, "I'll have your head!"

Once again, the miller's daughter considered her hopeless task and began to sob. No sooner had her tears begun to dampen the straw than the door opened and the strange little man hopped into the room.

"Why so sad, Mistress Miller?" he asked.

The young woman managed a weak smile for her tiny visitor. "Oh," she begged, "could you . . . I mean would you . . . spin all this straw into gold?"

"For a price!" he chortled. "A price! A price!"

The miller's daughter slipped the ring from her finger. "Will you do it for this?"

"Done!" he cried, snatching the ring from her outstretched hand. Then he sat beside the spinning wheel and worked all night, until every piece of straw had been spun into fine golden thread.

When the king opened the door the next morning, he gasped in delight at the sight of the gold. Yet he was still not satisfied. So that night he led the miller's daughter into an even larger room, filled to the ceiling with straw. "This is your final test," he declared. "If you spin all this straw into gold, I will marry you and make you my queen. But if you fail, I'll chop off your head."

When she was alone, the miller's daughter began to sob and sob, for she had never seen so much straw in her life. No sooner had her tears dampened the straw than the strange little man danced into the room. "A price!" he cried. "A price! I'll spin it for a price!"

"But I have nothing left," the young woman explained. "I've already given you my necklace and my ring."

"Then my price is a promise," he said. "When you become queen, you must give me your firstborn child."

The miller's daughter considered the offer. Perhaps she would never even have a child—and besides, what else could she do? "I promise," she vowed.

"Done!" crowed the little man. And by the first light of dawn, he had spun all the straw in the room into glittering, glistening golden thread.

When the king saw the huge room full of gold, his greedy heart was finally satisfied. *She's only a miller's daughter,* he thought, *but I couldn't find a wealthier woman in the whole world.* So the king and the miller's daughter were married in a joyous celebration, and the poor miller saw his dream of wealth and greatness fulfilled.

Time passed, and the beautiful queen gave birth to a beautiful child. As soon as mother and child were alone, the strange little man appeared and danced around the royal chamber. "My price! My price! I've come to collect my price!"

In the excitement of her new life, the queen had forgotten her promise. Now it all came back to her, and she was horrified by what she had done. "I will give you any treasure in the kingdom," she offered. "But please don't take my child."

"I don't want your treasure," snarled the little man. "A living thing means more to me than all the gold in the world!"

Clutching her baby, the queen began to sob, just as she had once sobbed over the piles of straw. Yet now she cried not for herself but for her precious child, and as her tears dampened the floor of the royal chamber, the strange little man felt sorry for her. "I will give you three days," he said. "If you can guess my name in that time, you may keep your child."

That night the queen lay awake, trying to remember every name she had ever heard. When the little man returned, she began with simple names like Jonathan, Ralph, and William. And when she ran out of those, she tried stranger names like Kaspar, Melchior, and Balthazar. But simple or strange, the little man just shook his head and said, "That's not my name."

On the second night, the queen racked her brain for names she had forgotten and tried to imagine names that the mother of a strange little man might give her strange little child. The next day, she offered each in turn. "Is your name Golden-nose?" she asked. "Dumpling-bottom? Spindle-sides?" But no matter how much imagination she used, the little man shook his head and said, "That's not my name."

That evening, the queen sat by the fire, rocking her baby in her arms, tears streaming down her beautiful face. She had run out of names, and now it seemed that she must give the horrible little man her firstborn child. Just then her husband, the king, came in from hunting and sat down beside her. "What's wrong, my dear?" he asked gently, for he had come to love her for herself as well as for her gold.

"Oh . . . it's nothing," she replied, wiping away her tears. "Just a change in the weather."

The king leaned back in his chair and laughed out loud. "I saw the most amusing thing today. In the middle of the hunt, deep in the woods, I came upon a tiny little cottage with a roaring fire in front of it. Around the fire danced a ridiculous little man, hopping on one foot and singing the silliest song:

"Today I brew, tomorrow I bake;
Soon I'll have the price I take.

Impossible to win my game,
For Rumpelstiltskin is my name!"

When the queen heard her husband's words, she nearly leaped from her chair in excitement. But instead, she held her child close and watched the roaring fire.

The next day, when the little man appeared in the royal chamber, she began by asking innocently, "Is your name Horatio?"

"That's not my name," he replied.

"What about Wilford?"

"That's not my name."

"Hmm. I don't suppose your name might be . . . Rumpelstiltskin?"

"A demon told you!" the little man screamed. "A demon! A demon!" He jumped up and down in anger, up and down, up and down—until, with a ferocious stomp, he drove his right foot through the floor of the chamber, sinking in the earth up to his waist. Then he pulled his left foot toward the ceiling with both hands and yanked so hard that he ripped himself in two . . . and disappeared.

The startled queen stared at the hole in the floor and felt a sharp twinge of sadness for the strange little man. From that moment on, she became the finest queen in the history of the kingdom, and it was said far and wide that she never made a promise she couldn't keep.

As for her father, the miller, he never learned the danger of foolish boasting. But then he never met Rumpelstiltskin.

"Rumpelstiltskin" was included in the first volume of the first edition of folktales by Jacob and Wilhelm Grimm, published in 1812 as Kinder-

und Hausmärchen (Children's and Household Tales). *The Grimms heard this story from two sisters, Dortchen and Lisette Wild, and their published tale combined the sisters' versions with some polishing by the Grimms. The Grimm and Wild families were quite close, and Wilhelm later married Dortchen Wild.*

Although "Rumpelstiltskin" is the most famous of this tale type, similar stories are told throughout Europe. The task is often spinning a large quantity of wool, rather than spinning straw into gold, and the magic helper may be a man, a woman, or a disgusting "thing." In England, the name is Tom Tit Tot or Terrytop, while in Scotland it's Whuppity Stoorie and in Wales Trwtyn-Tratyn. In Iceland, it's Gilitrutt, in Austria Kruzimügeli, in Hungary Winterkolbe or Panczumanczi, in France Robiquet or Mimi Pinson, in Italy Rosania, and in Russia Kinkach Martinko.

In this telling, I have generally followed the Grimms' tale, but I've added ideas from a version of "Tom Tit Tot" collected in Suffolk County, England, and first published in 1878. The most significant addition is that the king—rather than a messenger—happens upon the strange little man singing his song, which, to my mind at least, makes for a better story.

As folklorists Iona and Peter Opie pointed out in The Classic Fairy Tales, *"Rumpelstiltskin" works on many different levels. It is dramatic, moral, and fantastic. But at the heart of the story lies an ancient and deeply rooted belief found among many primitive peoples—the idea that a name carries power and magic.*

One-Inch Boy

Japan

An old, lonely couple longed for a child to share their simple life. So they went to the shrine of the Empress Jingo—for in those days, the spirits of the royal dead were worshiped as gods and goddesses.

"O mighty Empress," they prayed, "please grant us a child, even if it is no bigger than one of our fingers."

No sooner had the prayer left their mouths than a mysterious voice echoed from behind the bamboo screen. "Your wish has been granted. Go home and prepare."

Filled with joy, the couple returned to their humble home and prepared for the child to come. Nine months later, the old woman gave birth, just as the empress had promised. But the couple's joy became sorrow when they saw that the baby boy was no bigger than his mother's little finger.

"Perhaps he will grow," said the father.

"Perhaps," the mother agreed, but she couldn't help thinking that Empress Jingo had played a cruel joke.

The old couple named their son Issun Boshi. At first they treated him with love and kindness, hoping every day that he might begin to grow; but as the years passed—though Issun Boshi grew in his mind and heart and spirit—his body remained no bigger than his mother's little finger.

The people of the neighborhood made fun of the one-inch boy, calling him Little Finger, Bean Boy, and Grain of Corn. These insults stung his old parents, until finally they asked him to leave home and seek his fortune in the world.

"I will gladly go," he replied, eager for adventure. "I ask only for a sewing needle, a rice bowl, and a pair of chopsticks."

His parents gave him the things he requested, and he set off into the wide world, a one-inch boy with heart and spirit as big as a mountain. He slipped the sewing needle into a hollow straw and tucked them both beneath his belt, like a sword in a scabbard. The rice bowl he used as a boat and the chopsticks as oars, paddling down the long, sparkling river toward the royal city of Kyoto—home of the emperor.

When he reached his destination, Issun Boshi left his bowl and chopsticks beside the shore and wandered through the streets of the great city, gazing at the beautiful houses and temples and gardens. It was easy for the tiny boy to explore without being seen himself, for no one paid attention to a one-inch stranger. Finally he arrived at a house even more grand and beautiful than the others. Slipping between the bars of the outer gate, he walked right up to the front door.

"I beg an honorable audience!" he called, in a voice so tiny that the people of the house thought it was only the squeaking of a mouse. He called again and yet again, until the door opened and a great lord appeared, searching for the source of the tiny voice.

"Who's there?" he asked. "Who begs an honorable audience?"

"It is I," squeaked the visitor, "Issun Boshi."

The man looked around the courtyard, still searching for the source of the sound. But there was no one to be seen. He was about to return inside when he noticed the one-inch boy standing right beneath his feet. "Ah, there you are!" he exclaimed, a big smile spreading across his handsome face. "What brings you to the house of Prince Sanjo?"

Issun Boshi gasped in astonishment—he had found the home of Prince Sanjo, son of the emperor! Many common folk would shake with fright at coming face-to-face with such a powerful man, but Issun Boshi spoke with confidence. "Noble Prince," he said, "I have been sent away by my parents, and I ask to live in your house."

"Oh, you do?" the prince replied, laughing good-naturedly. "What can you offer me, Issun Boshi?"

The one-inch boy grasped the top of the sewing needle sticking out from the straw beneath his belt. "I can fight like the greatest samurai!" he claimed. "And I will defend your honor with my life. I'm also good at playing games."

Prince Sanjo rubbed his smooth cheek, as if he were considering the situation very seriously. Finally he said, "We can always use a brave samurai, and we have great need of game players. I am honored to accept you into my house."

17

So the one-inch boy joined the household of the great Prince Sanjo. With his brave heart and talent for games, he was assigned as a page to the prince's daughter, a beautiful young lady who was just about his age. Issun Boshi accompanied the princess wherever she went, and though he could barely see over her sandals, he always acted with great dignity, bringing honor to himself and to the family of Prince Sanjo. As the years passed, the princess grew very fond of her tiny servant, and the one-inch boy loved the princess in return.

One day, Issun Boshi accompanied Princess Sanjo to the Temple of Kannon, the goddess of mercy. As they were leaving the holy place, two terrible demons sprang upon them, threatening the princess with their deadly horns and tusks.

The one-inch boy grasped the handle of his sewing needle and pulled it out of the straw, waving its sharp tip at the brightly colored monsters. "Away!" he cried. "I am Issun Boshi and I protect the Princess Sanjo!"

The demons—one red, one blue—looked down at the tiny boy and burst out with cruel laughter. "Why, I could swallow you as a crow swallows a grain of corn," said the red demon. And without another word, he scooped the boy up and tossed him into his wide-open mouth. Issun Boshi slid down the huge throat and found himself in the creature's dark, disgusting stomach, surrounded by all the other things the monster had eaten that day. Yet even this did not frighten the brave little samurai. With the sharp tip of his needle-sword, he poked at the demon's stomach until the monster coughed a great cough that shot the tiny boy back out into the sunlit world.

Now the blue demon snarled with anger and tried to swallow Issun Boshi. This time, the little page was ready. He squirmed from the monster's grasp and climbed up into his nose, all the way to the place behind his eyeball. There he poked with his needle-sword until the demon sneezed a great sneeze that sent the boy flying out into the open air. Then the two horrible demons ran away, howling in pain, one holding his stomach, the other his bloody eye.

"Oh, Issun Boshi!" the princess exclaimed. "How can I repay you for such bravery?"

The one-inch boy bowed with great dignity. "No repayment is necessary. I am honored to protect you, noble Princess."

On the road home, Issun Boshi came upon a strange object blocking his path. It was made of wood, and to the tiny boy it looked like the trunk of a tree stuck into a stump. The princess reached down and picked it up with her delicate fingers. "What is it?" asked Issun Boshi.

"A mallet!" she replied, the excitement of discovery in her voice. "A magic wishing mallet! Those horrible demons must have dropped it."

"A magic wishing mallet?" asked Issun Boshi. Though he was a clever lad, he had never heard of such a thing.

"Yes," said the princess. "With a single strike of this hammer, any wish can be granted. Tell me, Issun Boshi, what do you wish?"

The one-inch boy gazed up at the beautiful princess. "I wish to grow taller," he said, "so that I may serve you even better."

Princess Sanjo bent down and tapped Issun Boshi lightly on the head with the magic mallet. "Grow taller," she commanded, "as tall as other men."

Before the startled eyes of the princess, the one-inch boy grew taller and taller and taller, until he stood as tall and handsome as the finest samurai in the land. "I am honored to serve you, noble Princess," he said, with a deep, respectful bow.

"Oh, my brave Issun Boshi," the princess sighed, "you need not bow to me. You are a man fit to serve the emperor himself."

And that is exactly what Issun Boshi did. But first he married Princess Sanjo, and the two of them lived happily ever after among the great lords and ladies of Japan.

––––––––

Issun Boshi is one of the most popular Japanese folktales. The basic idea is similar to "The History of Tom Thumb," the earliest folktale known to be published in the English language, with one printed text surviving from 1621. Tales of thumblings and finger-sized heroes are found in cultures all over the world, and folklore experts are undecided as to whether these stories are all different versions of the same original tale or whether some of them grew independently.

This retelling is based on a story published in 1913 in Myths and Legends of Japan, *by an English writer named F. Hadland Davis. Unfortunately, Davis did not provide sources for specific stories, but I would guess that it originally came from one of the block-printed pamphlets that Japanese mothers read to their children. Davis translated the name Issun Boshi as "One-Inch Priest," but the word "boshi" actually means "hat" in Japanese, so a literal translation would be "One-Inch Hat." More recent tellings usually give it as "Little One Inch."*

In 1910, three years before Davis's book was published, a government official named Kunio Yanagita began to collect oral tales from a farmer, opening the door to the careful study of Japanese folklore. By the 1950s, folklorists had collected more than fifteen thousand oral tales throughout Japan, including many different versions of Issun Boshi. At least one of these has been translated into English and is quite similar to the story told by Davis.

The demons in this story are oni, a nasty breed of monster who appear in many Japanese tales. They're similar to the European ogre— ugly, semihuman creatures with tusks and horns and supernatural powers. But unlike our flesh-colored monsters, the oni are brightly colored, usually red or blue. The magic mallet is also found in many Japanese stories, as is the old couple who long for a child to care for them in their old age. The samurai were the Japanese warrior class, men of honor and power. It seems only fitting that a tiny boy with a brave heart should become a samurai.

My Friend,
the Nisse

Denmark

There was once a small farm that could never keep a hired hand. The farmer paid the usual wages, with hearty meals and a comfortable bed in the hayloft. He was a fair master who asked no more than an honest day's work, and his wife was the best cook in the district. Yet the hired hands came and went as quickly as summer comes and goes in the cold, cold north.

One day a strapping young fellow named Hans appeared at the farmer's door looking for work. Hans had heard about the troubles at the farm, but he figured that one man's problem was another man's opportunity. Naturally, the farmer hired him in a minute and led him to the hayloft. "I hope you'll be happy here," he said. "The others, well . . ." The farmer just shrugged his shoulders.

Hans looked around the hayloft. It wasn't much—a bed of straw, a table with a lamp, a washbasin, and a single wooden chair. But it looked like home to him. "I'll be fine, sir," he replied. "See you in the morning."

By this time it was nearly dark, so Hans lit the lamp and prepared for bed. Just as he was pulling off his boots, he heard a scuffling sound in the barn below. Leaning over the edge of the hayloft, he watched a giant pile of hay enter through the barn door and move across the dirt floor—all by itself! Hans had seen many strange things in his life, but this was the strangest. At the far end of the wooden barn, the pile of hay came to a stop and landed with a soft *hiss* on the floor.

A tiny old man—no bigger than a child—emerged from under the load, straightening his red woolen cap and picking stray bits of hay from his gray beard with long gnarled hands.

Hans smiled to himself and nodded. Now he understood the troubles on the farm. It had a nisse, and a bad one at that. These nisse were everywhere, it seemed, on half the farms in Denmark. They were hard-working little fellows but full of mischief—this little devil had probably driven the other hired hands away with his pranks. *Well*, thought Hans, *I know a few pranks myself. I'll tease old Nis before Nis teases me.*

As the nisse perched on the pile of hay and lit his pipe, Hans sneaked down the ladder very quietly, tiptoeing through the shadows of the barn until he found a big pitchfork. Then he sneaked up behind the nisse and poked the fork through the hay, just hard enough to give him a good scare.

"Ahhhhh!" cried the little man, jumping down from the pile of hay and running round the dirt floor of the barn. "It pokes! It pokes!"

Standing in the shadows, Hans laughed out loud. "Ha! Two can play the pranking game, Nis!"

At the sound of the man's voice, the nisse stopped and squinted into the darkness. "Come out where I can see you," he demanded. When Hans stepped into the light, the nisse scrunched his face in disgust. "Hmmph! They've hired another big fellow. I don't see why they bother—I do all the work!"

Hans smiled broadly. "Well, I'm here now, Nis, and I plan to stay. Let that fork be a lesson to you."

"It wasn't one lesson," the nisse replied, "it was three lessons, for the fork had three prongs to poke me. And you shall be paid three times three!"

Hans laughed and climbed up the ladder to the hayloft, calling over his shoulder. "One, three, or three times three, it's all the same to me. Now it's time to sleep, Nis. We work in the morning."

The nisse said no more, but that night when Hans lay deep in sleep, the little old man climbed the ladder to the hayloft and lifted the hired hand out of his bed. Then he carried him out into the farmyard and tossed the big human right over the barn! Poor Hans woke up in midair, staring straight up at the sparkling Danish stars. Nis ran to the other side of the barn in time to catch Hans and throw him back again—and again and again, until Hans had flown over the barn nine times. Finally, Nis stepped aside and let the hired man land with a *plop* in a mud puddle right in the middle of the pigsty.

"Ha! Ha! Ha!" laughed the nisse. "Three times three is fun for me!"

Sitting in the mud puddle, surrounded by pigs, Hans realized that he had misjudged the little man. "Listen, Nis," he said, "let's be friends."

"Friends?" the nisse replied, scratching his long gray beard. "What is 'friends'?"

"Friends means I help you and you help me."

"Tell me more," requested Nis.

"To start with, we can share the hayloft. I'll make you a nice straw bed right next to mine. And I'll make sure you have hot porridge every night."

"With butter!" Nis demanded.

"With butter," Hans agreed. "One lump on weeknights, two lumps on Saturday, and three on Christmas Eve."

"I like this 'friends,'" said Nis. "And what do I do for you?"

"You help me take care of the farm."

"That's all?"

"That's all," said Hans.

The little gray-haired man stretched out his gnarled hand and pulled the big fellow out of the mud puddle. "Friends," he said with a smile.

From then on Hans and Nis had no more quarrels, and the little farm prospered as never before. But some time later a terrible famine gripped the land, and the piles of hay in the barn dwindled to almost nothing. Naturally, Nis went off to steal hay from a neighbor's farm. This was the nisse way, and though Hans suspected what his little friend was doing, he knew better than to ask questions. Yet no matter how much hay Nis stole, it seemed that there was never enough to feed the farmer's cattle.

Then one day, as Nis was carrying his load from the neighboring farm, he met another nisse on the road, carrying a load from his own farm. Now Nis understood—the other nisse was stealing from him as fast as he could steal himself!

"Hand me your hay!" Nis demanded. "It belongs to me!"

"Hand me *your* hay!" screamed the other nisse. "It belongs to *me!*"

The two nisses set their loads down and flew into each other like wild animals, fighting and biting and scratching. It was a terrible fight, but the neighboring nisse was stronger, and when it was over he carried both piles of hay to his own barn, while poor Nis limped home bloody and beaten.

"Nis!" cried Hans. "What's happened to you?"

As the hired man bathed his wounds, the nisse explained the whole story. "That other nisse is a bad one," he moaned. "I'm afraid he's too strong for me."

"Too strong?" Hans replied in disbelief. "Why, Nis, you threw me over the barn nine times!"

"You don't understand, my friend," Nis continued. "We nisse are stronger than human folk, but some nisses are stronger than others. That one will kill me for sure, unless . . ." His voice trailed off, as if he was lost in thought.

"Unless what?" asked Hans.

"Unless you help me."

"That's what friends are for," Hans assured him. "Just tell me what to do."

Late that night, Hans was awakened by a hissing wind outside the barn. He scrambled down the ladder and ran out into the farmyard, where he saw a big flaming wagon wheel rolling through the gate. Hans knew that this was the other nisse, coming to finish the battle. A moment later, a smaller flaming wheel rolled out of the barn—and Hans knew that it was Nis, come to fight for his life.

Hans grabbed the three-pronged pitchfork and watched the wheels battling back and forth, rolling and thrashing each other with their fiery spokes. The big wheel knocked the little one into a ditch, but Nis got up and attacked again. On and on the battle raged, until the big

wheel smashed the little wheel into the water trough, its flames sputtering and about to die. Moving quickly, Hans lifted Nis out with the pitchfork and tossed him back into the fight. But now his fire was weak, and the big wheel bashed him to the ground, pounding away and breaking his spokes. Just when it seemed that all was lost, Hans slipped the pitchfork into the big flaming wheel and heaved it high over the barn, where it shattered into shooting stars in the dark Danish sky.

As Hans stood sweaty and tired in the farmyard, Nis appeared in his old familiar form, his face blackened with soot, his gnarled hands wringing the water from his red woolen cap. "Thank you, my friend," he said.

From that day on, the little farm grew and prospered until it became the greatest and richest in the district, while the neighboring farm fell on hard times. The farmer always gave credit to Hans for his success, but Hans gave credit to Nis. And he never forgot to put out hot porridge with butter for his little friend—one lump on weeknights, two lumps on Saturday, and three on Christmas Eve.

I remember my own Danish grandmother telling me about the Julenisse *who brought Christmas presents to good children. (*Jul *is the Danish word for Yule or Christmas.) Even today the nisse is a symbol of Christmas in Denmark—although he faces competition from the* Julemand, *or Christmas Man, known in America as Santa Claus. But this connection between the nisse and Christmas is relatively recent. Two hundred years ago, the nisse was a farm spirit who cared for the animals and made sure the barn was full of hay. All he asked in return was a bowl of hot porridge with butter.*

Although the Danish nisse has a special character of his own, similar stories are told of the Norwegian nisse and the Swedish tomte. He is also similar to other household spirits of northern Europe, including the kobold of Germany, the brownie of Scotland, and the hobgoblin of England. All of these creatures help humans who treat them with proper respect, but they can be cruel and mischievous to those who don't. The name nisse comes from Niels (Nicholas in English), and Old Niels is a Danish nickname for the Devil, as is Old Nick in English. In earlier times, Christian ministers called the nisses fallen angels or lost souls, an idea that reflects their attitude toward "pagan" beliefs—for the nisse and other domestic spirits seem to be direct descendants of Viking house gods and ancient Roman gods of house and field.

This story is based on a variety of sources, including oral tales that were collected from the old people of rural Denmark during the nineteenth century by folklorists J. M. Thiele and Evald Tang Kristensen. I have also used a delightful book published in 1889 by the Danish writer Vilhelm Bergsøe, who wove the oral tales collected by Thiele, Kristensen, and others into his own literary work. A slightly shorter version of Bergsøe's book (originally entitled Nissen*) was translated into English by Virginia Allen Jensen as* The Nisse from Timsgaard. *Although I'm indebted to these sources—and many others—I used my own imagination to create a story that is both old and new.*

(I would like to thank my cousin Charlotte Kunst, who is a children's librarian in Denmark, for helping me research the nisse and translating some Danish sources. I also thank Virginia Allen Jensen for explaining her work in translating Bergsøe's book and Danish folklorist Iørn Piø for providing me with an English translation of his study of the nisse, which includes a number of the early oral tales.)

The Capture
of Summer

North America

I n the long ago time, when people lived only in the red light before sunrise, the great Lord Glooskap walked toward the north until he reached a land of endless ice and snow. There he came upon a huge wigwam and entered, looking for a place to rest and warm himself by the fire. But he found no roaring fire inside—only the towering giant of Winter.

"Come and smoke awhile, Lord Glooskap," offered the giant, "and I will tell you tales of the old times."

Now Glooskap was fond of smoking, for he himself had brought tobacco to the earth. And he was fond of a good story, too, for many a tale told of his adventures and generous gifts. So he took the pipe from the giant's outstretched arm and seated himself comfortably on the floor of the wigwam.

As Glooskap smoked, Winter spoke of the old times, his voice slow and deep and sleepy. "In the long ago, a giant blew his breath, and streams . . . stood . . . still. He shook his white hair, and snow . . . covered . . . all."

Soon Glooskap fell under the spell of Frost, unable to move from his place. Yet still Winter spoke, even slower and deeper and sleepier, until the giant froze and Glooskap slipped into a deep and dreamless sleep.

For six months, Glooskap slept like a toad in the lodge of Winter. Then the spell wore off, and he rose to leave the giant's wigwam. He walked toward his home, and with each southward step, the air grew warmer and the flowers began to grow and speak to him—the lord of men and beasts.

In time he came to an opening in the forest, where golden shafts filtered through the trees. There, in a glowing circle of laughter, the fairies of light danced around their tiny queen. She was Summer, the most beautiful ever born, as delicate and graceful as a flower dancing in the warm west wind. As Glooskap watched her turn and twirl, tossing her long black hair like summer rain, his heart felt laughter, too. And so he formed a plan to avenge himself on Winter and help the people who lived in the red morning and the others to come, the ones who would live in the bright light of day.

From the hide of a moose, the Master cut a thin cord, so long that it would stretch from the place the sun rises to the place that it sets. He made a loop in one end of the cord and tiptoed across the clearing, so quietly that the dancing fairies never noticed his approach. Then, like a flash of sunlight, he slipped the loop over Summer, scooped her up in his hand, and ran toward the north, the cord trailing behind

him. Though she struggled to escape, the iron grip of Glooskap was too strong. And though the fairies of light grabbed the trailing cord, pulling mightily to rescue their queen, the cord ran out farther and farther still, until Glooskap had left them far behind.

While the Great One ran through the northern woods, the tiny, outraged voice of Summer rose from within his hand. "How dare you kidnap me! Release me and return me to the south!"

"Not yet, my little queen," he replied softly. "I am Glooskap, the one who made you and all the fairies of light. Soon enough you will rule among them. But first I need your warmth."

Once again Glooskap came to the land of ice and snow, and once again the giant of Winter welcomed him into the wigwam, hoping to freeze him with sleepy tales of Frost. "Come and smoke awhile," the giant offered, "and I will tell you more stories of the old days."

"I will gladly smoke," Glooskap answered, "but this time *I* will tell the tales."

Taking the pipe from the giant's outstretched hand, the Master seated himself comfortably on the floor of the lodge, the tiny queen of Summer held close against his chest. Glooskap spoke of the old times, his voice as light and lively as laughter. "In the long ago, a fairy queen blew her sweet breath, and flowers opened. She shook her long black hair, and warm rain fell upon the earth."

As Glooskap told his tales, the heat of Summer filled the giant's lodge. Soon Winter began to sweat, salty drops running down his face like a river flooding in the spring. Still Glooskap spoke, even lighter, more lively with laughter. When Winter fought to blow his last cold breath, Glooskap released Summer and set her dancing on the earth, shaking her raven hair, twirling like a flower in the warm west wind, until Winter melted away and the wigwam melted with him.

Now the world around them awoke, and everything came to life: flowers, trees, and grass; beasts of the forest and birds of the air. The snow flowed into rivers, and rivers washed away dead leaves. When the land looked fresh and new, the fairies of light came out to dance, and Glooskap left Summer to be their queen, just as she had been in the south.

"Lord Glooskap!" Summer called, her tiny voice carrying through the sweet, warm air. "It was good you brought me here, but there was no need to steal me. I would have come freely—if you had asked."

Glooskap stood among the tall trees, smiling at the graceful dancer in her circle of light. "I will remember that, my queen. Now and forever."

And so it was that Summer came to the north.

Glooskap is the culture-hero of the Wabanaki people, a group of related tribes in what is now the northeastern United States and southeastern Canada. The Wabanaki credit Glooskap with a wonderful variety of gifts and adventures—from the creation of little folk, people, and animals to battles with evil sorcerers and a ride on a talking whale. Unlike Coyote, the culture-hero of many western tribes, Glooskap is almost always noble and helpful to mankind, only playing tricks on those who ask unreasonable favors.

The story of Glooskap and the capture of Summer was first published in 1884, in The Algonquin Legends of New England *by Charles G. Leland, who collected more than two hundred tales from three Wabanaki tribes: the Passamaquoddy and Penobscot of Maine and the Micmac of New Brunswick, Canada. This particular tale was originally sung as a story-poem by an Indian named Neptune and written down by Mrs. W. Wallace Brown, the wife of a missionary among the Passamaquoddy. Mrs. Brown then shared it with Leland.*

The Wabanaki are part of the widely spread Algonquian language group, with tribes ranging from northern Canada to the southern United States, and from the Atlantic Ocean to the Rocky Mountains. A similar story, told by the Algonquian-speaking Ojibway of northern Minnesota, was published in 1839 in Algic Researches *by Henry Rowe Schoolcraft. In this version, Summer is a young man who melts old-man Winter with his tales. I have borrowed a bit of the tales from the Ojibway, since they are only suggested in the Wabanaki story.*

Little people appear in the folklore of many Indian tribes, and they are often described as living among the rocks—a characteristic of little folk all over the world. But the tale of Glooskap and the tiny queen of Summer is a different kind of story, a nature myth explaining the changing seasons. For the Wabanaki, who live in a land of long, harsh winters and short, mild summers, it was natural to imagine Winter as a great giant and Summer as a fragile fairy queen.

People of the Rock

South Africa

Long ago in the land of the Zulu, a husband and wife had many cattle and rich stores of grain. Yet their hearts were sad, for they had no children. They went to the tribal doctors and drank mysterious potions, but still no child came to fill their home with joy. And so the years passed and their sorrow grew.

Then one day the wife announced that she was expecting a baby. The couple counted the days, waiting for the great moment; but when it arrived, the shadow of sorrow darkened their hearts again. For there was not one child, but two—a boy and a girl. Twins. In those days, the Zulu believed that twins brought disaster to the land, and Zulu custom required that twins be put to death at birth.

"What shall we do?" the father wailed. "How can I kill my own children?"

"Look at them," murmured his wife, cradling the newborn babies in her arms. "So beautiful, so sweet and innocent. We must protect them."

"Yes," he agreed. "We will hide them as two and show them as one."

That is exactly what they did. They named the boy Demana and the girl Demazana; yet whenever visitors came only one child appeared. Perhaps it was Demana, perhaps Demazana. The other remained hidden from the eyes of the village.

At first the trick worked well, but as the babies grew into a little boy and girl, it became more difficult to pretend that the two were one. So the family moved far away from the village, to the banks of a wild river that raced through a rocky gorge.

Beyond this gorge was a great dome-shaped rock that was split down the middle, as if it had been struck by lightning. There was another, smaller crack as well, so the Zulu called it the Rock of Two Holes. They believed that horrible cannibals lived inside its walls, for they had heard strange songs echoing in the night. Some even said the rock opened and closed like a door at the command of magic words. No one came near the Rock of Two Holes if they could help it.

For a time the family lived together in safety and happiness. Then, when the twins were six years old, disaster struck the land of the Zulu. Cattle died and crops wilted in the fields. Cries of sickness and hunger filled the villages and reached the ears of the Zulu king, who called his tribe together and spoke from the royal throne.

"There is evil in the land," he announced. "Tomorrow I will send my doctors out among you. They will smell the evil, and the guilty will be punished."

The king's words filled the parents of Demana and Demazana with fear. "We cannot hide them," their father whispered. "We must do the deed ourselves."

Their mother nodded her head and wiped the tears from her eyes. "Do what you must," she replied.

That afternoon, Demana and Demazana accompanied their father to the wild river, thinking they were going to draw water for drinking. When they reached the river's edge, he threw them into the raging torrent, one after the other. Then, holding his hands over his eyes so he wouldn't see them sink, he stumbled blindly up the bank and back to the family's house—the house that once again had no children.

But the twins did not sink. Instead, as the river rushed through the rocky gorge, they fought for life with a power beyond their years. Demana clawed his way to the surface and grabbed on to a branch that arched out from the shore. He pulled himself from the water, and then—with the strength of a brother's love—he pulled Demazana out as well. Carefully, they worked their way along the branch and collapsed in exhaustion on the shore, just beneath the Rock of Two Holes.

As the sun warmed their cold, wet bodies, the twins heard a strange creaking and watched in amazement as the Rock opened like a magic door. Soft, soothing songs echoed from within, and a troop of tiny singers filed out into the sunshine and circled the twins on the shore.

"We are nunus," they sang. "Welcome to our home. Come inside and live with us. All sad hearts are mended here."

Demana and Demazana rose from the ground and eagerly followed the little nunus into the Rock of Two Holes. When the great

door closed behind them, they discovered a huge domed cavern lit by the soft light of glow worms and fireflies. It was a place of love and kindness, where the nunus healed all the sad and injured creatures of the world: tiny beetles with broken legs and an eagle with a broken wing; lizards who had lost their tails and a baby fawn who had lost its mother to the lion's claws. All were welcome here, and all lived together in peace.

The little twins needed healing, too, for their hearts were broken by the treachery of their parents. So they stayed with the nunus in their hidden world, living on mushrooms that grew along the rocky walls and wild honey that trickled in from a beehive on the outside. When the children needed sunshine, the nunus taught them the magic words that would open the door of the Rock:

> *Rock of Two Holes, open for me!*
> *Rock of Two Holes, open for me!*
> *If you will not open for me,*
> *Open for the swallows that fly in the air!*
> *Rock of Two Holes, open for me!*

With these words, the twins could run and play along the river whenever they wished and still return to the hidden safety of the Rock. It was a happy life, and in time Demana and Demazana forgot about their parents. But their parents did not forget the twins. Every day they grieved for the little ones they had lost because of their own fears. And every day their father prowled the riverbank, praying that somehow they had escaped the wild and deadly water.

Then one day he saw them—splashing and laughing in a little

pool near the Rock of Two Holes. Running quickly along the shore, he wrapped them in his powerful arms and greeted them with gentle words. "We have missed you so," he said. "Come home with me to your mother."

"Who are you?" asked Demazana.

"Why, I am your father," he replied, staring strangely at the little girl. "Don't you recognize me?"

Demana stood bravely between his sister and the older man. "We have no father," he declared. "We are people of the Rock."

Their father begged and pleaded, explaining all that had happened, from the birth of the twins to the threats of the Zulu king and the horrible moment when he threw his own children into the river. "I am so sorry," he told them. "Please come home. Your mother's heart is broken."

Demana and Demazana understood the pain of a broken heart, and they agreed to follow their father back to their mother's arms. Yet though she gave them all her love, the children soon grew restless, longing for their nunu friends and the other creatures of the Rock. So one dark night, as their mother and father slept, Demana took Demazana by the hand, and they walked back along the riverbank to the Rock of Two Holes. There, in two soft voices that sounded as one, they sang the magic words:

> *"Rock of Two Holes, open for me!*
> *Rock of Two Holes, open for me!*
> *If you will not open for me,*
> *Open for the swallows that fly in the air!*
> *Rock of Two Holes, open for me!"*

While their song lingered in the cool night air, the great Rock opened and the little nunus came out to greet them. "Welcome home, Demana and Demazana," they sang. "We have missed you so!"

Grasping their tiny hands, the twins followed their friends into the magical place of healing and safety. And there they live to this day, helping the nunus care for all the sad and injured creatures of the world.

The Zulu live in a region called KwaZulu, near the northeastern coast of the Republic of South Africa. They were a relatively small group until 1818, when the great King Shaka forged them into an awesome military force that conquered many of the surrounding tribes. Later, the Zulu resisted the expansion of white settlement, and today they play an important role in the changing politics of South Africa.

The Zulu have a rich tradition of storytelling, often told around the fire by the older women. This tale is based on a story that was published by a white South African writer named Phyllis Savory in 1961 as part of a collection called Zulu Fireside Tales. *In her introduction to the book, Savory indicated that she heard some of the stories from her young Zulu maid, Duduzele, and the others from Duduzele's mother.*

I was unable to find earlier texts of this specific story or other tales about the nunus. However, South African folklorist Cicely van Straten wrote to tell me that nunus are "small, shy creatures that live on the fringes of human society. . . . They seem to be mainly friendly, but a little unpredictable, and a naughty child can be gently threatened by calling up the nunus." Ms. van Straten explains that the nunus are not usually thought to be humanoid, and it's difficult to see them clearly, though you might feel their presence or glimpse them on the move.

I did discover several other stories about the Rock of Two Holes, including two Zulu versions published in 1868 and a tale from the neighboring Xhosa people published in 1882. In all these stories, the same magical incantation is used to open the rock, and in the Xhosa tale, the brother and sister are called Demane and Demazana. But instead of the kindhearted nunus who heal the creatures of the world, the rock is home to terrible cannibals who try to steal the girl. Personally, I prefer the nunus.

(I would like to thank Phyllis Savory's son, T. L. Willson, and the Struik Publishing Group for giving me permission to retell the story "Ntunjambili," which originally appeared in Zulu Fireside Tales. *Thanks, as well, to Cicely van Straten and Jay Heale for their South African insights.)*

The Golden Ball

Wales

Elidyr looked up from his book and gazed out at the distant river, winding through the countryside. *The river runs free,* he thought, *yet I am held in walls of stone.* Before he could think again, the boy felt the hard *thwack!* of his teacher's rod across his shoulders—for in those days, long ago, teachers were not so pleasant as they are today.

"The book!" the teacher demanded. "The book, not the window!"

Elidyr nodded meekly and looked back at the open page, trying to decipher the handwritten Latin words. It was no use. He was tired of learning, tired of school, tired of the rod. A moment later, when the teacher turned his back, the boy slipped out the door and ran for the river. There he hid beneath the hollow bank just beyond the rushing water, with nothing to eat for two long days.

45

On the second day, when Elidyr's stomach ached with hunger, two tiny men appeared outside his hiding place. They were handsome fellows, perfectly formed, with fair skin and long, flowing hair. "If you come with us," they offered, "we'll show you a land of sports and games."

"Will there be food?" Elidyr asked.

"As much as you desire."

The boy eagerly crawled out from under the bank and followed the little men, first along the river, then through a long, dark underground passage. Finally they emerged into a beautiful land of gentle rivers and green meadows, lush forests and broad open plains—all cast in a hazy twilight where the sun never shone.

The two little men guided Elidyr to their king, who stared at the tall human boy for a long, long while. "Who are you," he asked finally, "and where do you come from?"

"My name is Elidyr, Your Majesty, and I come from a place called Wales."

The king stroked his long, shimmering hair. "Ah yes, we know this Wales. It is in the world of sunlight, where you humans lie and steal and think only of yourselves."

Elidyr was shocked by the king's description of human ways, and he wanted to defend his race. But his tongue fell silent, for he knew that it was true.

"Tell me," said the king more kindly, "do you like to play?"

The boy's face brightened with joy. "More than anything!"

"Good. For that is all we do when we are not eating or sleeping. You can play with my son as long as you like. But I warn you, human boy, we are a gentle, honest people. We worship Truth as you worship God in the world above. Do you understand?"

Elidyr nodded his head. "I understand."

With a warm smile, the king motioned to a tiny, handsome boy about Elidyr's age. "Come, my son, and take our guest to the kitchen. He must be starving after his long journey. And when he has eaten, you may play and play and play!"

In the royal kitchen, Elidyr discovered that the little people ate neither meat nor fish, but only milk custard flavored with saffron. It was delicious, and the tiny prince watched with wide little eyes as the human boy gobbled bowl after bowl until he was full. Then they ran out to play in the beautiful fields and forests of the twilight land.

They played many games: hide-and-seek, tag, and jousting on horses no bigger than greyhounds. But their favorite game was ball— a perfect ball of solid gold that they rolled and chased through the soft green meadows. Elidyr had never seen such a ball before, and he asked where it had come from.

"It's nothing," said the prince with a shrug. "We have so much gold that any child can have a golden ball. Catch!"

At the end of the day, an inky darkness covered the land, for there were no moon or stars to light the night. The next morning, Elidyr and the young prince rushed out again into the hazy twilight for hours and hours of play. And so it went, day after day, until one day the human boy remembered his mother. "She must be very worried," he told his playmate. "I would like to see her."

"Of course," the prince replied. "I'll tell my father."

That afternoon, the two little men who had first found Elidyr beside the river guided him back through the long, dark passage and into the world of sunlight.

"You may visit us whenever you wish," they said. "Now you know the way."

In the months that followed, Elidyr traveled freely between the world of twilight and the human world above. He spoke of his journeys to no one except his mother, but to her he told everything: the appearance of the little people, their love of truth and play, their customs and their food, their plentiful supply of gold. It was the gold that interested his mother most, and she asked him to bring back a gift.

"After all," she pointed out, "these wee folks have more than they need."

Elidyr was eager to please his mother after causing such grief by running away. So the next morning he returned to the twilight world and played as usual with the tiny prince. Then late in the day, as they rolled the golden ball through the soft green meadow, he scooped the toy up in his hands and ran toward the long, dark passage.

"My ball!" the prince shouted. "My golden ball!"

Looking back over his shoulder, Elidyr saw the two little guides in hot pursuit, running as fast as their legs could carry them. He sprinted through the darkness and out into the sunlit world, but still they followed, scrambling up the riverbank behind him and running at his heels all the way to his mother's house. As he burst through the doorway, Elidyr tripped and sprawled into the room; the golden ball slipped from his grasp and rolled out the door, just in time for one of the guides to scoop it up with his tiny hands.

"Human!" he snarled, spitting out the word as if it were a curse. Then the two little men turned away and walked back toward the river.

On the floor of his mother's house, Elidyr recovered his breath and realized what a horrible thing he had done. "You should not have asked me, Mother," he muttered sadly. "And I should not have listened." Rising slowly to his feet, he stumbled out the door and followed the path of the little men, hoping to beg their forgiveness. But when he reached the river, the entrance to the dark passage had disappeared. There was only the muddy, overgrown bank.

For nearly a year, Elidyr returned to the river every day, searching for the entrance to the twilight world. He searched in the place he remembered and in places he could only imagine, but he never found the passage again.

Time passed, and Elidyr drifted back to his old way of life and his old school, where he studied as he had not studied before. He grew up to become a learned priest, a man of books and God, respected and loved by all who knew him. Yet even in his old age, Father Elidyr's eyes grew damp with tears whenever he spoke of the twilight world.

This story was reported in a twelfth-century travel book entitled The Journey through Wales, *written by a clergyman called Gerald of Wales. In the spring of 1188, Gerald accompanied the Archbishop of Canterbury on a tour of Wales, aimed at raising support for the Third Crusade. This was the same crusade that took Richard the Lionhearted away from England, allowing his brother Prince John to grab power—a historical situation that plays such an important part in the legend of Robin Hood.*

Much of Gerald's book is devoted to accurate descriptions of the people, places, and scenery that they encountered along the way, and modern scholars still consider it an important source for medieval Welsh history. The experience of Elidyr is casually dropped into a description of events in Swansea on the southern coast of Wales. "Sometime before our own time," Gerald begins, "an odd thing happened in these parts. The priest Elidyr always maintained that it was he who was the person concerned."

Apparently, Gerald never met Elidyr, but his uncle, Bishop David FitzGerald—the leading clergyman in Wales—spoke with the old priest several times about his experience and even learned many details of the little people's language. Gerald gives specific examples of their words and launches into a serious comparison of the language with Greek and Welsh. Although he presents the story as history, Gerald admits that he's not quite sure what to make of it: "If, careful reader, you should ask me if I think that this story of the little folk is true, I can only answer with [Saint] Augustine that 'miracles sent by Heaven are there to be wondered at, not argued about or discussed.'"

Laka and the Menehune

Hawaiian Islands

Chief Wahieloa ruled on the island of Maui long before we were born. He was a man of perfect royal blood— the thirty-first chief in his family—and on Maui the gods of his ancestors watched over him as the wind watches over the waters.

When it came time to marry, Wahieloa wed the beautiful Hina-hawea, whose own people came from the big island of Hawaii. The wedding was celebrated with feasting and dancing and chanting that lasted for many days.

In time Hina expected a child, so Chief Wahieloa crossed the deep blue water to the home of his wife's people, in search of a birth gift. But on the island of Hawaii, his family gods could not protect him, and Wahieloa was killed by an evil one who threw the chief's body into a cave guarded by a wicked old woman named Kaikapu.

A short while later, the child was born—a beautiful boy with eyes that shone like sunlight glistening upon the waves. His mother named him Laka, and he grew to be a fine young man, stronger than all of his playmates. When he defeated the other boys at sports and games, they taunted him with cruel words, chanting, "Laka has no father! No father! No father!"

Stung by these insults, Laka asked his mother to tell him of his father. Her heart still ached with sorrow, so she sent him to her own mother, a woman wise in the ways and wonders of the world.

"Grandmother," Laka asked, "who was my father, and what has become of him?"

In a voice kind with wisdom, the old woman told of the great Chief Wahieloa and how he crossed the sea for a birth gift and never returned. "Oh, my grandson," she said sadly, "I have heard that he was killed on my own island, the island of Hawaii, and that his bones lie restless in a cave guarded by the wicked Kaikapu. If this be so, you must cross the sea and bring them back to Maui, where the gods of his ancestors—and your ancestors—will watch over them for all time."

"But how will I cross the sea, Grandmother?"

"You must build a great double canoe, big enough and strong enough to ride the thundering waves."

"And how will I build such a canoe?"

"Go to the mountains, my grandson, and find a tree with leaves shaped like the new moon."

Following his grandmother's advice, Laka journeyed into the dense mountain forest, where he found a tree with leaves shaped like the crescent of the newborn moon. With his sharp stone ax, he cut

the huge tree down and left it on the forest floor, for night had cast its shadows across the mountain world. Yet when Laka returned the next morning, the tree stood upright and alive in the place where he had found it!

Puzzled by this moving tree, Laka chose another tree with crescent leaves of the new moon. All day he worked with his sharp stone ax, and again he left the fallen tree on the forest floor. But when he returned, this tree too stood upright and alive. So he chose yet another tree and chopped it down, only to find that it rose in the night just as the others before it. Finally Laka spoke of the mystery to his grandmother.

"You must dig a hole in the forest floor," she told him, "big enough to hold the tree. And when the tree has fallen into the hole, you must climb in beside it and lie in wait for those who will come."

Laka did as his grandmother instructed, and that night, when dark shadows covered the mountain world, he hid beside the huge tree with crescent leaves of the newborn moon. Suddenly he heard countless voices chanting, at first in the distance, then closer and closer still. And these were the words of the chant:

> *Oh, the four thousand gods,*
> *The forty thousand gods,*
> *The four hundred thousand gods,*
> *The file of gods,*
> *The assembly of gods!*
>
> *Oh gods of these woods,*
> *Of the mountain,*
> *And the hill,*
> *At the water dam,*
> *Oh, come!*

From his place behind the tree, Laka watched in wonder as the forest filled with little men, no taller than his knees, yet sturdy and strong. When they began to lift the tree, he leaped up and grabbed two of them in his hands, holding tightly and shaking them in anger. "Who are you," Laka cried, "to raise the tree I cut for my double canoe? I should kill you for my trouble!"

"We are Menehune," one of the little men replied, "and if you spare us, we will build your canoe in a single night."

"A single night?" Laka asked. "How can that be?"

"It is always so with us," explained the other, "for we work together in all we do, and we never do the same job twice. That is why we say, 'In one night and it is finished.'"

"But you must do something in return," added the first Menehune. "Build a shed on the beach, big enough to hold the great canoe, and when we bring it down from the mountains, you must feed us for our labors."

"Gladly," Laka replied, and he released his grip on the two little men, setting them softly on the ground.

Now all the Menehune gathered around, staring curiously at the tall stranger. "Tell us," they asked. "What is your name? And who was your father?"

"I am Laka, son of Wahieloa."

At these words, the hum of Menehune voices filled the forest, the little men speaking among themselves so quickly and quietly that Laka could not understand. "What is it?" he asked. "What are you saying?"

The chief of the Menehune—the one whom Laka had first caught beside the fallen tree—stepped forward to explain. "We knew your father well," he said, "for Wahieloa was son of Kaha'i, who was son of Hema, who was son of Ai-kanaka, who descended from us. So you, too, Laka, have Menehune blood. That is why you can see us, for we only appear to our relatives. And that is why we will build your canoe. Now go home, make all ready, and return tomorrow evening."

The next day, Laka built a shed on the beach and helped his grandmother prepare a feast for the little men. Then he returned to the mountain forest and found two huge and perfect canoes resting side by side—carved by the Menehune in a single night. When

darkness crept across the forest floor, the little men appeared, telling Laka to go home and wait, for they would bring him the double canoe by dawn.

All that night, Laka lay awake in his grandmother's house, listening to the sounds of the dark island. When he heard a faint humming in the distance, he knew that the Menehune were lifting the canoes. When he heard a stronger humming, he knew that they were carrying the canoes down the steep mountain path. And when he heard a loud humming outside his door, he knew that the Menehune were placing the canoes in the shed on the beach. Then Laka rose from his bed and found the great canoes waiting to be lashed together and launched on the deep blue water.

Now Laka and his grandmother spread a feast for the little men— the green leaves of the taro plant and a single shrimp for each. When they had eaten their fill, just before dawn, the Menehune filed off toward their home high in the mountain forest, chanting as they left:

> *"Oh, the four thousand gods,*
> *The forty thousand gods,*
> *The four hundred thousand gods,*
> *The file of gods,*
> *The assembly of gods!"*

As the sun rose over the water, Laka lashed the two canoes together and prepared to launch them into the waves. Just then, his wise old grandmother appeared. "I have brought you four helpers," she announced. "Prop, Reach, Torch, and Seeker. When you find the cave of your father's bones, you must offer the wicked woman a bowl of soup. These men will do the rest. Now go, my grandson."

Laka and his four helpers paddled across the deep blue water in the great double canoe of the Menehune. When they reached the big island of Hawaii, they found the cave where his father's bones were held, but the entrance was closed with solid rock. "Oh, Grandmother Kaikapu," Laka called sweetly, "if you open the door, we will give you a delicious bowl of soup."

The rock opened and the hideous face of Kaikapu filled the entrance. "Where's the soup?" she demanded. "I'm starving!"

Laka handed the old woman a bowl of steaming soup, but after a single taste she screamed, "More salt!" and slammed the rock shut.

Now Reach stretched across the waves, bringing salt back from every sea in the world, until finally a sea was found whose salt was strong enough for the taste of Kaikapu. "Delicious!" the old woman murmured, eagerly slurping the salty soup from the bowl. In an instant, Prop held open the mouth of the cave, Torch lit the darkness, Seeker found the bones of Wahieloa, and Reach pulled them out and handed them to Laka. Then they sealed the cave and left wicked Kaikapu to slurp her soup in the dark.

When Laka returned to Maui, he buried his father's bones in a secret cave, along with the great double canoe. To this day, no one has ever found that cave, but many have seen the hole in the forest floor where Laka hid when he first saw the little men. And everyone knows that Laka became the thirty-second chief of his family and that he always honored his relatives, the Menehune, who carved his canoe in a single night.

The Menehune play an intriguing role in Hawaiian myth and legend, similar in many ways to the little people of European folklore. They are said to be the original inhabitants of the islands, expert craftsmen who always completed their labors in a single night. But most of the Menehune left the islands long ago, leaving only a few stragglers behind, who hid away in caves and hollow rocks. In the early twentieth century, Hawaiians still pointed out various structures on the islands that were said to be built by the Menehune.

The story of Laka and the Menehune is part of a larger cycle of tales about five chiefs in the long line of chiefs who were claimed as ancestors by the rulers of Hawaii and Maui. A similar cycle of tales is found among many other islanders of the South Pacific, including the people of Tahiti and the Maori of New Zealand. In these cycles, Laka is called Rata, and the details of his adventures vary, but the basic story remains the same.

I have based this retelling on a version of the Laka story published in 1907 by Thomas G. Thrum in Hawaiian Folk Tales, *a collection of stories and essays that had originally appeared in Thrum's* Hawaiian Almanac and Annual. *The almanac began publication in 1875, but Thrum didn't indicate when or where he first heard the Laka story. Thrum's version stops with the delivery of the great canoe, so I've added the description of Laka's voyage—as well as additional details about Laka and the Menehune—from various sources summarized by folklorist Martha Beckwith in* Hawaiian Mythology.

The Red-Ribbon Leprechaun

Ireland

Bridget Rooney went out one morning to draw water from the local well. Now Bridget was a pretty colleen—which is an Irish word for a girl—and she had a good head and heart, too, not to mention a strong right arm. Someday she hoped to marry Darby Riley from over the hill, but Darby was a poor boy and Bridget was poorer still. So their marrying plans had to wait until they could work their way up in the world.

On the way to the well, Bridget was walking on the sunny side of a thornbush when she heard a *tap, tap, tap* in the clear Irish air. She stopped in her tracks, set her water pitcher on the ground, and ever-so-careful peered into the bush—where what did she see but a tiny old man no bigger than her boot tops, tapping away at a tinier shoe that no one could fit but himself! He wore a three-cornered hat with

golden lace, a leather apron, and breeches that came to his knees. With a pipe in his mouth and a jug at his side, he was so busy working and singing an Irish tune that he didn't even notice Bridget watching him from above.

By all the saints, she thought, *'tis a leprechaun for sure! If I'm careful and quick, my fortune is made—and Darby's fortune, too!*

Fast as the wind, Bridget grabbed the leprechaun and squeezed him tight. "B'gore and b'gone!" he screeched. "Let a body breathe!" Bridget eased her grip a bit, but she never took her eyes off the little man—for taking your eyes off a leprechaun is the surest way to let him escape.

"Ah, that's better," he said, looking up at the girl who held him in her power. "You'd think a pretty colleen like yourself would have better to do than pester a poor old shoemaker."

"Poor, my eye," Bridget replied. "It's your gold I'm after, Mr. Leprechaun, and I mean to have it."

"Oh, gold, is it?" asked the leprechaun innocently. "Why, I haven't a penny in the whole wide world."

"It's more than pennies you've got," said Bridget, "and if you don't show me where you've hid your gold, you'll be sorry you ever met Bridget Rooney." With that, Bridget twisted her pretty face into a wicked, bloodthirsty scowl and gave the little man a hard squeeze with her strong right hand.

"All right, Bridget Rooney!" he gasped. "You're too strong and clever for the likes of me. I'll show you a crock of gold if you just let me breathe."

"That's a good fellow," said Bridget, relaxing her grip but keeping the little man locked in her hand. "Now show me the way."

With the leprechaun as her guide, Bridget walked past the well through farms and fields, across hedges and ditches, until they were out in the wild countryside. It seemed like the leprechaun was taking the longest and hardest path he could, just to pay her back for making him give away his gold. But Bridget walked where he told her to walk, never taking her eyes away for an instant. They were heading down a gentle valley when the leprechaun pointed behind them and shouted, "Look, Bridget! It's Darby Riley comin' over the hill!"

"Darby! Where?" Bridget was about to turn and look, but she caught herself just in time, keeping an eye on the little man and giving him a good hard squeeze to remind him what was what and who was who. "Oh, Darby Riley, is it?" she said with a scowl. "Well, maybe it is and maybe it isn't, but you won't get away so easy from Bridget Rooney. Now show me the gold."

"You're a hard one, Bridget, that's for sure," the leprechaun admitted. "But come along now. It's just over the next hill."

Bridget carried the leprechaun over the hill and gazed out over a great field of ragweed—acres and acres of bushes, every one of them the same. The leprechaun guided her through the ragweed, until they came to one that looked no different than the others. "Dig under this bush," he said, "and you'll find a whole crockful of gold."

Suddenly Bridget realized that she'd forgotten to bring a shovel, so she had nothing to dig with but her bare hands. She decided to run home and fetch a good digging spade, but first she set the little man on the ground. Then she loosened the red ribbon from her hair and tied it around the ragweed bush, so she would know the place again.

"I suppose," said the leprechaun politely, "that you have no more need for my services."

"No," Bridget replied, just as politely. "I don't. And I wish you good luck wherever you go."

"Well, good-bye to you, Bridget Rooney," muttered the leprechaun, scampering away through the field of ragweed. "And much good may it do you, with what you'll get."

Bridget ran all the way home, over the hills, across the ditches, and through the fields and farms, thinking of the gold that lay waiting beneath the bush. Why, she and Darby would live like lord and lady in a big house with beautiful things and never a care in the world! What a life it would be!

Without a word to anyone, she grabbed the spade and ran back again, past the well, through the farms, and over the hills, until she came to the great field of ragweed. What did she see but ten thousand bushes, every one of them tied with a red ribbon just like the ribbon

from her hair! She could no more tell one bush from another than she could tell one grain of sand from another on the shore. And as for digging under every bush, why, she would be long dead—and her children and her children's children, too—before the task was done.

With her shovel on her shoulder, Bridget Rooney walked back home, and a long, sad walk it was. She found her water pitcher beside the thornbush and peeped into the place where she had first seen the little man, but there was no sign of him or the tools of his shoemaking trade. So she dipped her pitcher into the well and brought it home to her mother, as she had set out to do in the first place.

Now the story's a sad one but not so sad as some, for Bridget Rooney married her Darby Riley, and they lived to a ripe old age with children and grandchildren galore. They had to work for their money just like everyone else, and they never lived like lord and lady in a big house with fancy things, but their house was happy just the same.

As for the leprechaun—no one ever saw him again in the thornbush, but some say they still hear his *tap, tap, tap* in the clear Irish air.

The leprechaun is perhaps the most famous and well loved of all the little folk. Today, most people think of leprechauns as delightful little creatures who advertise breakfast cereal and play harmless pranks on St. Patrick's Day. But in the early nineteenth century—when the people of the Irish countryside believed that leprechauns were part of daily life—they were considered rather nasty fellows who played cruel tricks and would stop at nothing to keep humans from getting their gold.

This story is based on several nineteenth-century sources. The basic tale of the leprechaun who covered a field of ragweed with red ribbons was originally published by T. Crofton Croker in 1825. Croker was the first folklorist to gather stories from the Irish countryside, and though he retold them in a more literary style, he tried to remain true to the oral tales. In his story called "The Field of Boliauns," the trick is played on a young man named Tom Fitzpatrick, and the red ribbon is a red garter used to hold up Tom's socks. I also drew on various tales in which a young man or woman captures a leprechaun and then loses him when he tricks the human into looking away. The names Bridget Rooney and Darby Riley for two young sweethearts are from another Croker leprechaun story, as well as an old Irish song.

In the early nineteenth century, the leprechaun was known by many names in different regions of Ireland. For example, in the southern county of Cork, where Crofton Croker did his research, he was called the cluricaune, while in the eastern county of Kildare he was the lurikeen. Croker believed that all of these names referred to the same creature and that they were based on the Old Irish word for a pygmy, literally "small body." Most modern scholars agree, but the word is also quite similar to the Irish term for "one shoe"—which led to the idea that leprechauns were shoemakers for the fairies.

Bibliography

Author's Note

Evans-Wentz, W. Y. *The Fairy-Faith in Celtic Countries.* "The Smallness of Elvish Spirits and Fairies," pp. 233–44. New York: Carol Publishing Group, Citadel Press, The Library of the Mystic Arts Edition, 1990; 1st ed., 1911.

Rumpelstiltskin

The following are translations of "Rumpelstilzchen" by Jacob and Wilhelm Grimm, first published in *Kinder- und Hausmärchen,* Berlin, 1812, and included in subsequent editions.

The Complete Fairy Tales of the Brothers Grimm. Translated by Jack Zipes. Story 55, "Rumpelstiltskin," pp. 209–12. New York: Bantam Books, 1987.

Grimms' Tales for Young and Old: The Complete Stories. Translated by Ralph Manheim. Story 55, "Rumpelstiltskin," pp. 196–98. Garden City, NY: Doubleday & Co., 1977.

Grimms' Fairy Tales. Based on the Frances Jenkins Olcott edition of the English translation by Margaret Hunt, first published 1922. [Hunt translation first published 1884.] "Rumpelstiltskin," pp. 279–84. Chicago: Follett Publishing, 1968.

Household Stories from the Collection of the Brothers Grimm. Translated by Lucy Crane. "Rumpelstiltskin," pp. 228–31. New York: Macmillan and Co., 1886. Reprint, New York: Dover Publications, 1963.

Lang, Andrew, ed. *The Blue Fairy Book.* [Translated by May Sellar.] "Rumpelstiltzkin," pp. 96–99. Longmans, Green, and Co., c. 1889. Reprint, New York: Dover Publications, 1965.

"Rumpel-Stilts-Kin." From *German Popular Stories.* Edgar Taylor, ed. London: 1823. Reprint, with an introduction by Iona Opie and Peter Opie, eds., comps., in *The Classic Fairy Tales,* pp. 195–98. Oxford: Oxford University Press, 1974.

Tom Tit Tot

A. W. T. [Mrs. Walter-Thomas.] "Suffolk Notes and Queries," *Ipswich Journal,* 15 January 1878. Reprint, in "The Philosophy of Rumpelstiltskin" by Edward Clodd. *The Folk-Lore Journal,* 1889. Reprint, in *An Encyclopedia of Fairies* by Katharine Briggs. s.v. "Tom Tit Tot." New York: Pantheon Books, 1976.

One-Inch Boy

Davis, F. Hadland. *Myths and Legends of Japan.* Ch. XXX, "The Transformation of Issunboshi, and Kintaro, the Golden Boy," pp. 364–67. London: G. G. Harrap, 1913. Reprint, New York: Dover Publications, 1992.

Mayer, Fanny Hagin, ed. and trans. *The Yanagita Guide to the Japanese Folk Tale.* No. 8, "Issun Boshi," pp. 11–13. Bloomington, Ind.: 1986.

Seki, Keigo, ed. *Folktales of Japan.* Translated by Robert J. Adams. No. 28, "Little One Inch," pp. 90–92. Folktales of the World. Chicago: University of Chicago Press, 1963.

My Friend, the Nisse

Bergsøe, Vilhelm. *The Nisse from Timsgaard.* Translated by Virginia Allen Jensen. New York: Coward, McCann & Geoghegan, 1972. Originally published as *Nissen.* Denmark: Ernst Bojesens Kunstforlag, 1889.

Briggs, Katharine. *The Vanishing People: Fairy Lore and Legends.* Chapter 4, "House Spirits," pp. 53–65. New York: Pantheon Books, 1978.

Keightley, Thomas. *The World Guide to Gnomes, Fairies, Elves, and Other Little People.* "Nisses," pp. 139–47. Originally published as *The Fairy Mythology.* London: G. Bell, 1878; 1st ed. 1828. Reprint, New York: Avenel Books, 1978.

Kunst, Charlotte. Personal correspondence 1994–95, including translation of flaming wagon wheel story from Evald Tang Kristensen. *Danske Sagn,* Vol. 2. Aarhus, Denmark: 1893.

Kvidelund, Reimund, and Henning K. Sehmsdorf, eds. *Scandinavian Folk Belief and Legend.* No. 48, "The Spirit of the Farm," pp. 238–45. Minneapolis: University of Minnesota Press, 1988.

Olsen, Ib Spang. "The Christmas Nisse in Denmark." Copenhagen: The Press and Cultural Relations Department of the Ministry of Foreign Affairs, n.d.

Piø, Iørn. *The Nisse: Traditional Danish Farm-Goblin.* Translated by Johannes Knudsen. Printed privately. Originally published as *Nissen.* Copenhagen: Gyldendals Forlag, 1980.

THE CAPTURE OF SUMMER

Leland, Charles G. *The Algonquin Legends of New England; or, Myths and Folk Lore of the Micmac, Passamaquoddy, and Penobscot Tribes.* "How Glooskap Found the Summer," pp. 134–36. Boston: Houghton Mifflin, 1884. Reprint, *Algonquin Legends.* New York: Dover Publications, 1992.

Schoolcraft, Henry Rowe. *Algic Researches: Indian Tales and Legends.* Vol. I. "Peboan and Seegwun. An Allegory," pp. 84–86. New York: Harper & Brothers, 1839. Reprint (2 vols. in 1), with introduction by W. K. McNeil, Baltimore: Clearfield Co., 1992.

Spence, Lewis. *The Myths of the North American Indians.* "How Glooskap Caught the Summer" and "The Elves of Light," pp. 147–49. London: G. G. Harrap, 1914. Reprint, New York: Dover Publications, 1989.

PEOPLE OF THE ROCK

Callaway, Rev. Canon [Henry]. *Nursery Tales, Traditions and Histories of the Zulus.* "The Rock of Two-holes; or, The Cannibal's Cave," pp. 140–41; "The Girl and the Cannibals," pp. 142–52. Springvale, Natal: John A. Blair, 1868. Reprint, Westport, Conn.: Negro Universities Press, 1970.

Savory, Phyllis. *Zulu Fireside Tales.* "Ntunjambili," pp. 9–14. Cape Town: Howard Timmins, 1961.

———. *Bantu Folk Tales from Southern Africa.* "Ntunjambili," pp. 15–19. Cape Town: Howard Timmins, 1974.

Straten, Cicely van. Personal correspondence, Sept. 26, 1995.

Theal, George McCall. *Kaffir Folklore: A Selection from the Traditional Tales Current among the People Living on the Eastern Border of the Cape Colony.* 2d ed. "The Story of Demane and Demazana," pp. 118–21. London: Swan Sonnenschein, Le Bas and Lowrey, 1886; 1st ed. 1882.

THE GOLDEN BALL

The following are translations of the story as reported in the Latin manuscript *Itinerarium Kambriae (The Journey through Wales)* by Giraldus Cambrensis (Gerald of Wales). Gerald revised this manuscript three times; the first version was probably completed in 1191, the second in 1197, and the third in 1214. The story of Elidurus (Elidyr) is the same in all three versions.

Gerald of Wales. *The Journey through Wales and The Description of Wales.* Translated by Lewis Thorpe. Book 1, Ch. 8, pp. 133–36. Harmondsworth, England: Penguin Books, 1978.

Geraldus [sic] Cambrensis. "The Adventure of Elidurus." In Thomas Crofton Croker, *Fairy Legends and Traditions of the South of Ireland,* Part III, pp. 240–42. London: John Murray, 1828. Reprint (3 vols. in 1), New York: Lemma Publishing Corporation, 1971.

Giraldus Cambrensis. *The Itinerary through Wales.* Translated by R. C. Hoare. pp. 390–91. Bohn Library, 1863. Reprint in Katharine Briggs, *The Vanishing People: Fairy Lore and Legends,* pp. 157–58. New York: Pantheon Books, 1978.

LAKA AND THE MENEHUNE

Beckwith, Martha. *Hawaiian Mythology.* Ch. XVII, "Aikanaka-Kaha'i Cycle," pp. 238–58; Ch. XVIII, "Wahieloa-Laka Cycle," pp. 259–75; Ch. XXIII, "Mu and Menehune People," pp. 321–36. New Haven: Yale University Press, 1940. Reprint, with introduction by Katharine Luomala, Honolulu: University of Hawaii Press, 1970.

Colum, Padraic. *At the Gateways of the Day.* "The Me-ne-hu-ne," pp. 149–64. Tales & Legends of Hawaii, vol. 1. New Haven: Yale University Press, 1924.

————. *The Bright Islands.* "The Story of Rata the Grandson of Tawhaki," pp. 103–18. Tales & Legends of Hawaii, vol. 2. New Haven: Yale University Press, 1925.

Thrum, Thomas G. "Stories of the Menehunes." In *Hawaiian Folk Tales: A Collection of Native Legends.* 3rd ed., pp. 107–17, compiled by Thomas G. Thrum. Chicago: A. C. McClurg & Co., 1917, c. 1912; 1st ed. 1907.

THE RED-RIBBON LEPRECHAUN

Briggs, Katharine. *An Encyclopedia of Fairies.* s.v. "Lepracaun." New York: Pantheon Books, 1976.

Croker, Thomas Crofton. *Fairy Legends and Traditions of the South of Ireland.* [Part I.] "Seeing Is Believing," pp. 169–80; "The Field of Boliauns," pp. 199–210. London: John Murray, 1825. Reprint (3 vols. in 1), New York: Lemma Publishing Corporation, 1971.

————. *Fairy Legends and Traditions of the South of Ireland,* A New and Complete Edition edited by Thomas Wright. "Seeing Is Believing," pp. 85–90; "The Field of Boliauns," pp. 102–7. London: William Tegg, 1862.

Hall, Mr. and Mrs. S. *Ireland: Its Scenery, Character &c.* 3 vols. London: Hall, Virtue, 1850; first pub. 1841–43. Vol. 3, pp. 35–37. Reprinted as "Jack and the Cluricaune" in *Irish Folk Tales,* pp. 162–64. Edited by Henry Glassie. New York: Pantheon Books, 1985.

Kennedy, Patrick. *Legendary Fictions of the Irish Celts.* "The Kildare Lurikeen," pp. 130–31. London: Macmillan and Co., 1866. Reprint, Detroit: Singing Tree Press, 1968.